Conductors and Insulators Electricity Kids Book

Electricity & Electronics

BABY PROFESSOR
EDUCATION KIDS

Speedy Publishing LLC
40 E. Main St. #1156
Newark, DE 19711
www.speedypublishing.com
Copyright 2016

Electricity is useful in our everyday lives. We are able to do things more easily because of the flow of electricity in our appliances at home.
But do you know how electricity flows?

Well, it flows because of Conductors and Insulators. But what is the difference between a conductor and an insulator? Can you give examples for each?

After this discussion, you will be able to differentiate and give examples of a conductor and an insulator.

A conductor is
a material that
conducts electricity
because of its
free electrons.

What is an electron?

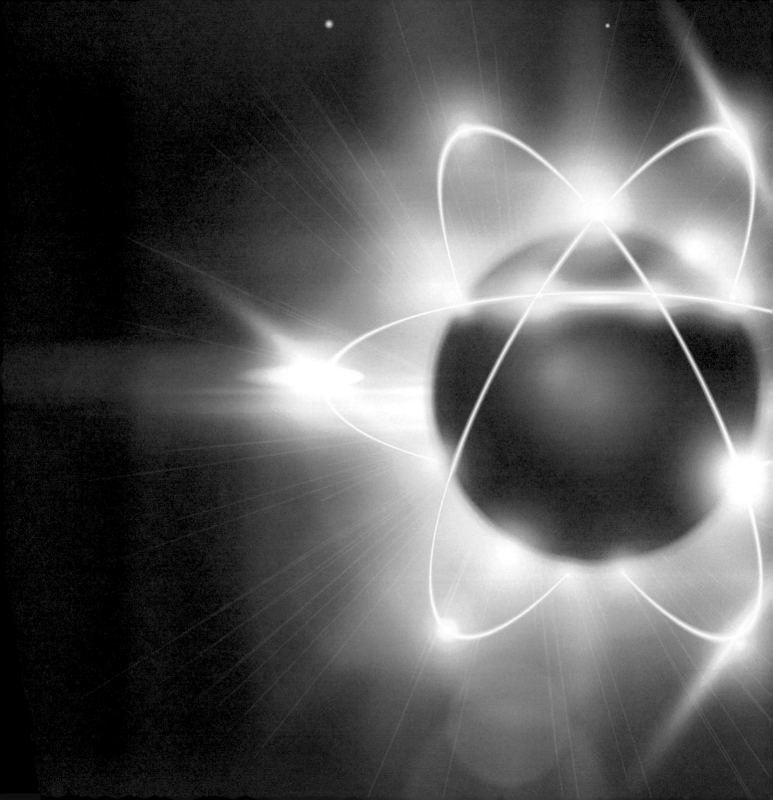

An atom is made
up of electrons,
protons, and
neutrons. We can't
see them because
they are too small.

Protons and neutrons are particles that can be found in the center of an atom known as the nucleus. Both are small but electrons are much smaller. Electrons are outside the nucleus, spinning around it.

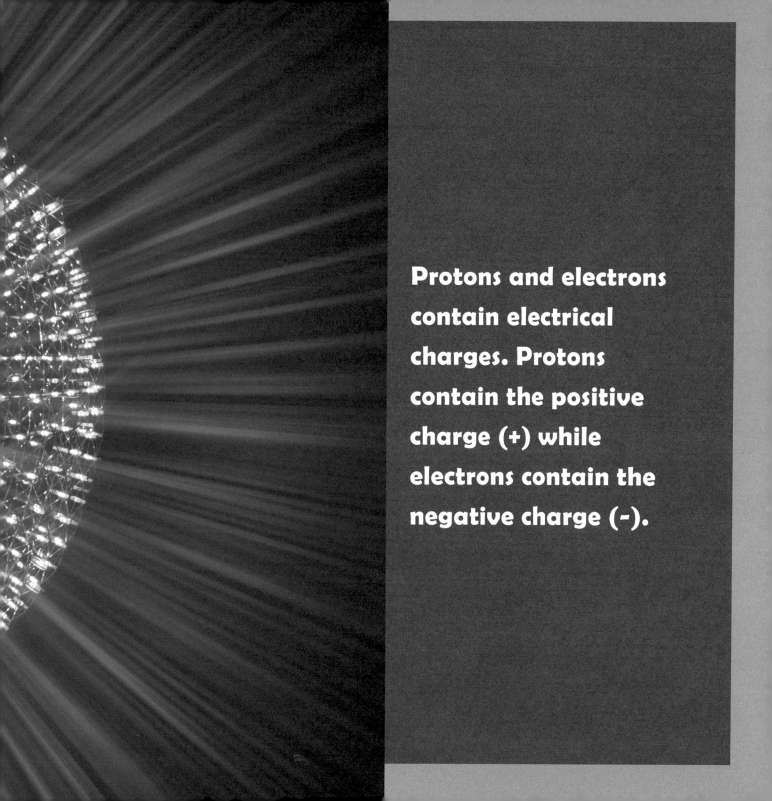

Protons and electrons contain electrical charges. Protons contain the positive charge (+) while electrons contain the negative charge (-).

Neutrons, on the other hand, don't contain any charge. Protons and electrons are attracted to each other. An amount of protons in an atom is equal to the amount of electrons.

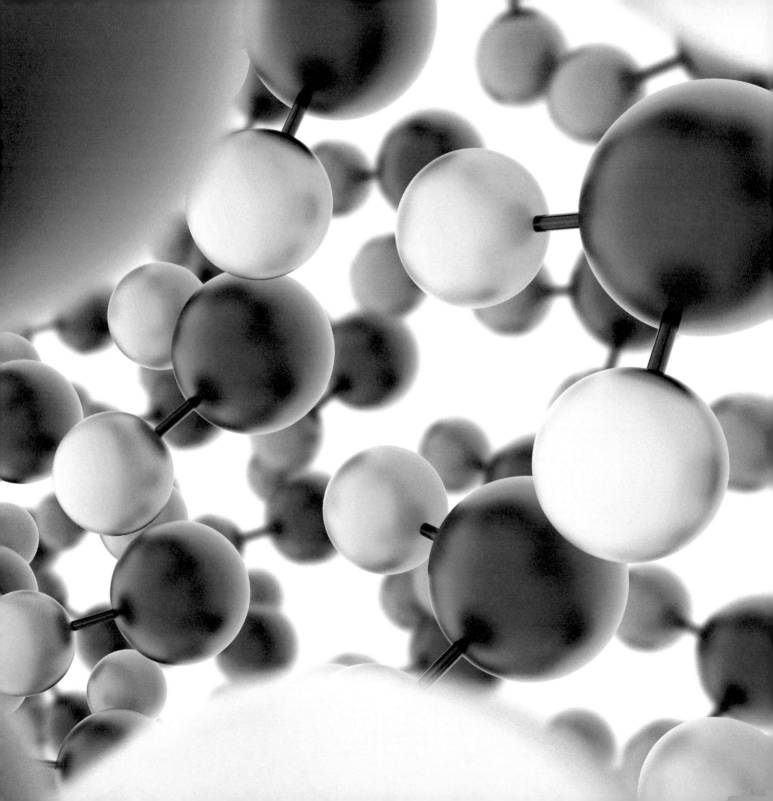

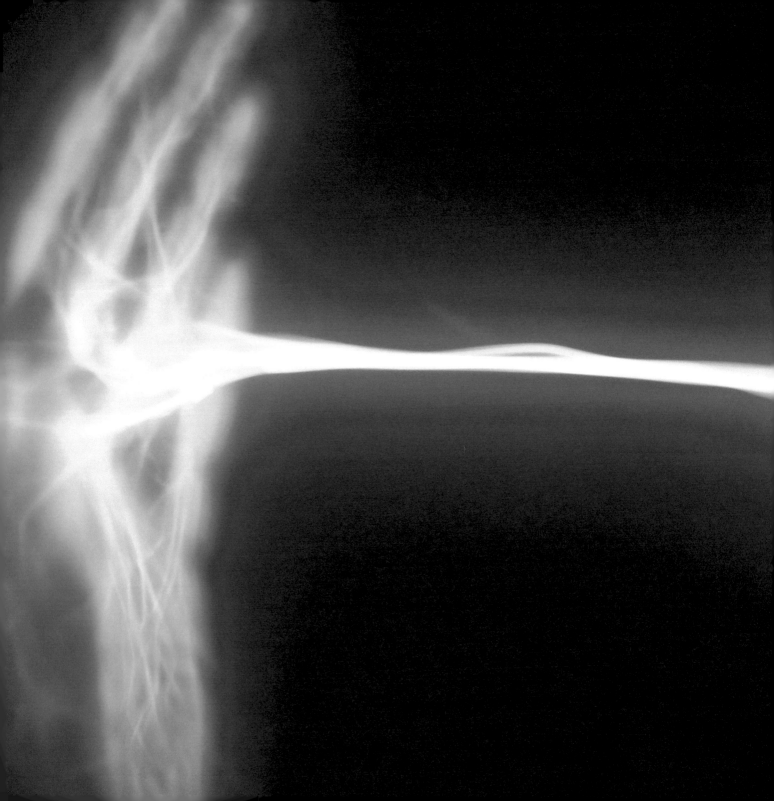

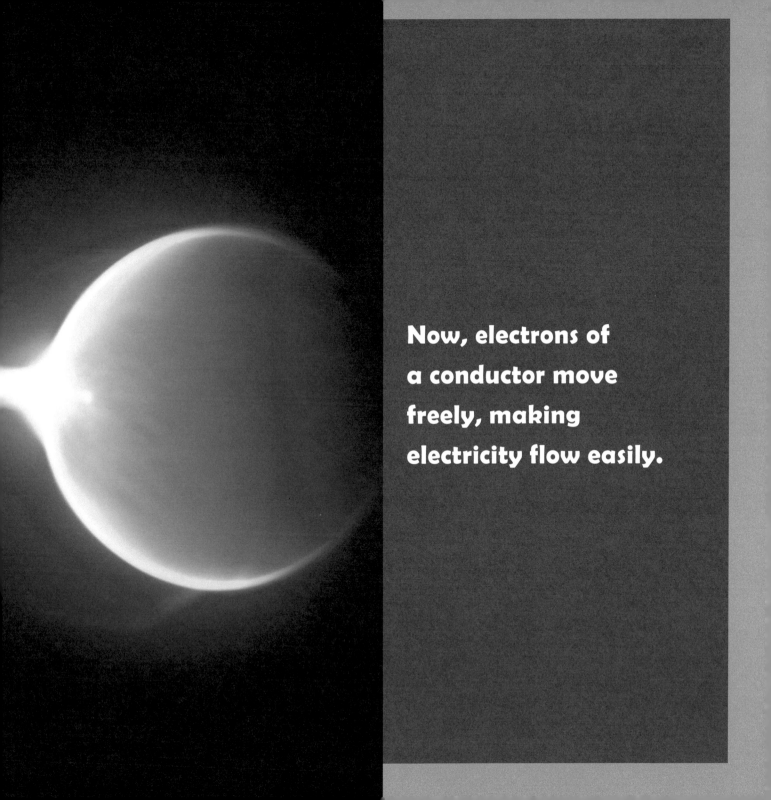

Now, electrons of a conductor move freely, making electricity flow easily.

There are several good electrical conductors.

Do you know what those are?

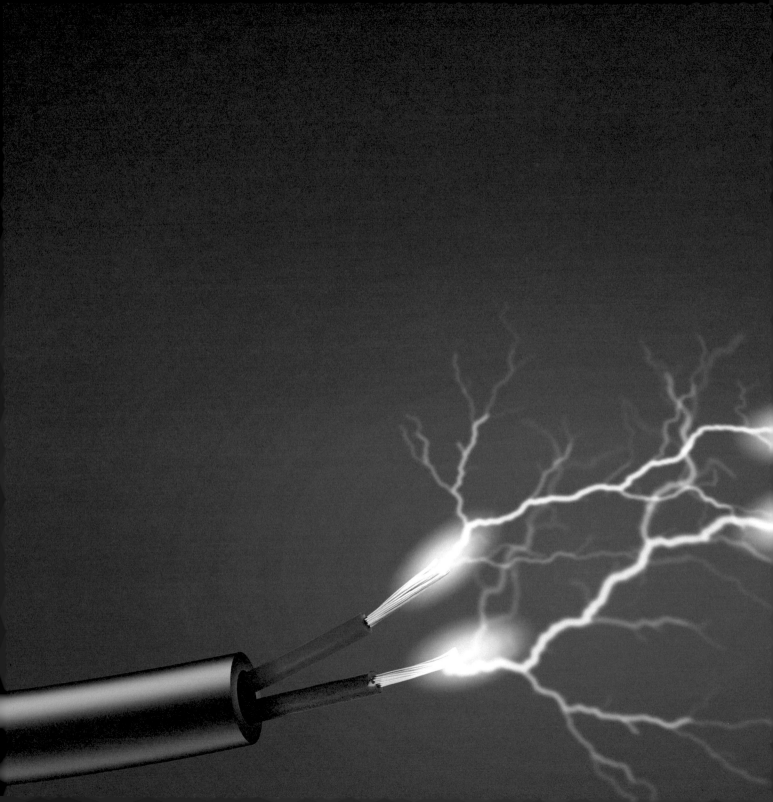

**Electrical conductors
include:**

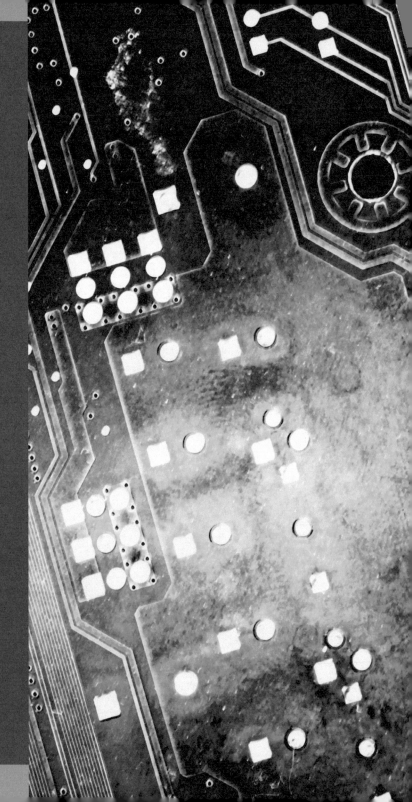

Gold - can conduct
heat and electricity.

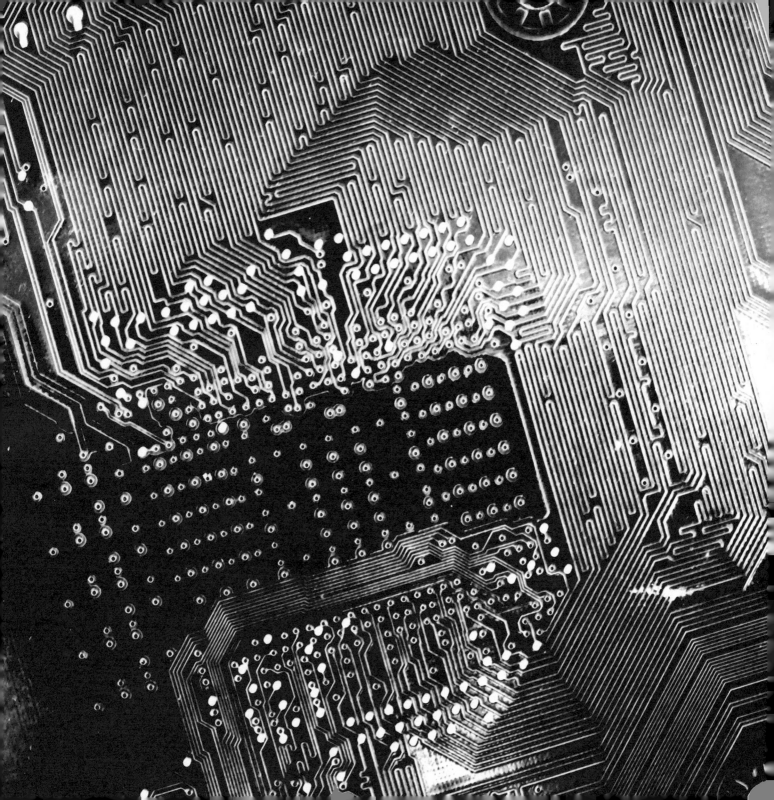

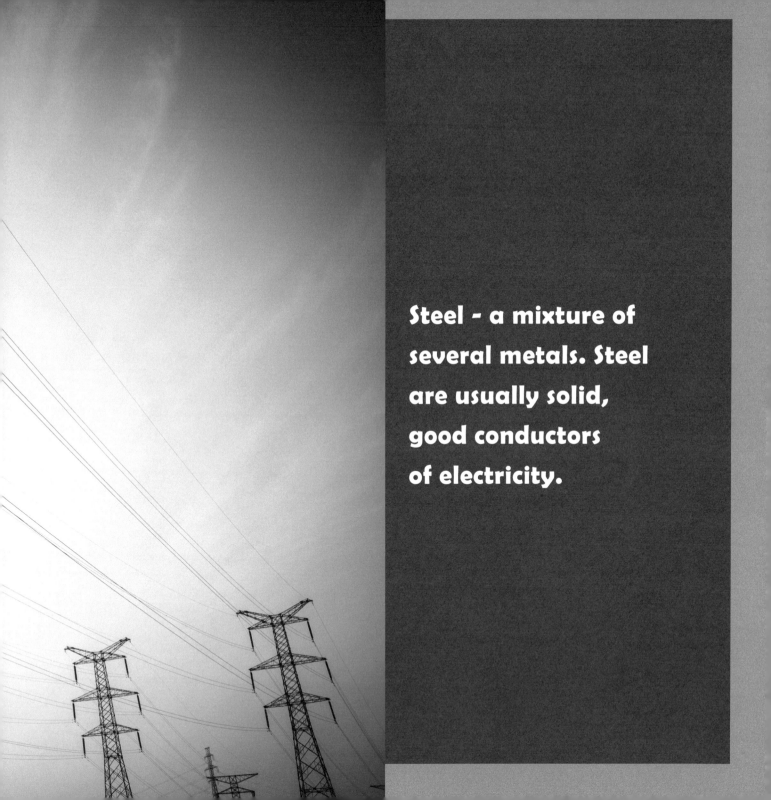

Steel - a mixture of several metals. Steel are usually solid, good conductors of electricity.

Copper - a chemical
element with
the symbol "Cu".
Copper is found
in TVs, radios,
washers, dryers and
some cookware.

Iron - the most
widely used metal
in the world.

Mercury - the most abundant element in the Earth.

As you have noticed, most of the good electrical conductors are metals. One of the best electrical conductors is copper. Gold and silver are also good conductors, even better than copper, but they are expensive and are not often used.

An insulator is the material that keeps us safe from electricity. It is very important so that we will be far away from the harmful effects of electricity like getting an electric shock. We don't want that to happen.

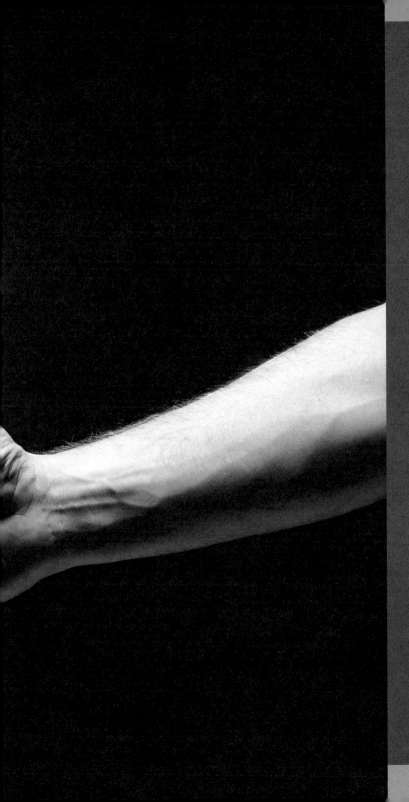

The rubber-like covering that you can see around the wire of your appliances is the insulator. An insulator is the exact opposite of a conductor because it doesn't carry electricity.

Here are examples of electrical insulators:

Dry Wood - dry wood works well as an insulator because of all the empty space that it contains.

Plastic - Plastic's properties as an electrical insulator also make it useful for wrapping wires.

Rubber is a good insulator. It is used on the outside of wires that are used to conduct electricity.

The use of paper as electrical insulation started in the twentieth century.

The earliest glass insulators were used to insulate lightning rods and cables from structures.

Have you noticed
the telephone poles
that carry phone lines
to all the houses? It
is made of wood.

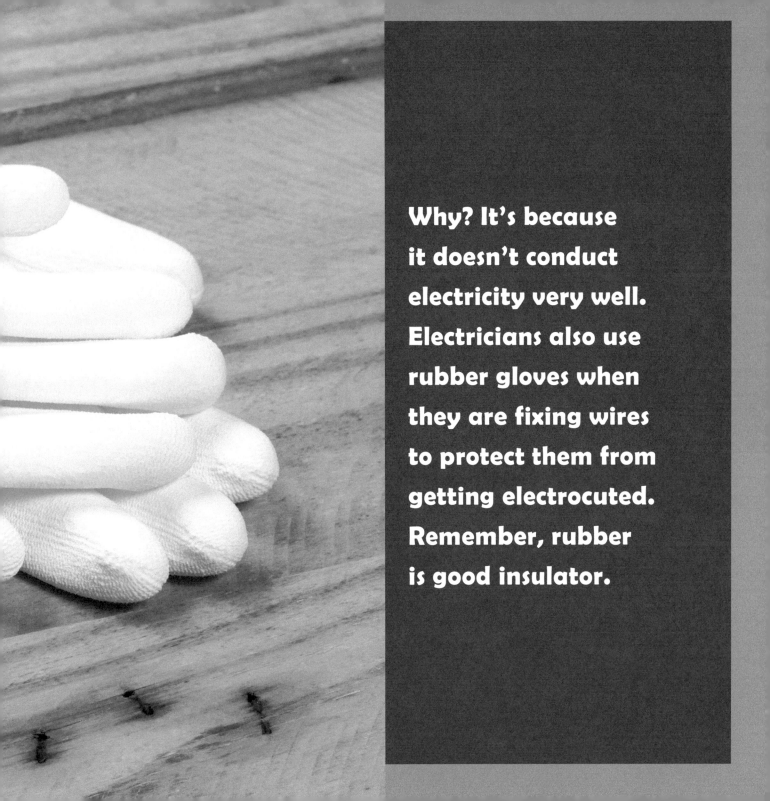

Why? It's because it doesn't conduct electricity very well. Electricians also use rubber gloves when they are fixing wires to protect them from getting electrocuted. Remember, rubber is good insulator.

Aside from conductors and insulators, there is also what we called semi- conductors. These materials are important in electronics like the mobile phones and computers that we use every day.

Semi-conductors' conductivity is in between conductors and insulators. Silicon is a good semi-conductor. It partly conducts electricity.

Knowing the difference between conductors and insulators helps us understand how electricity travels and powers up our homes.

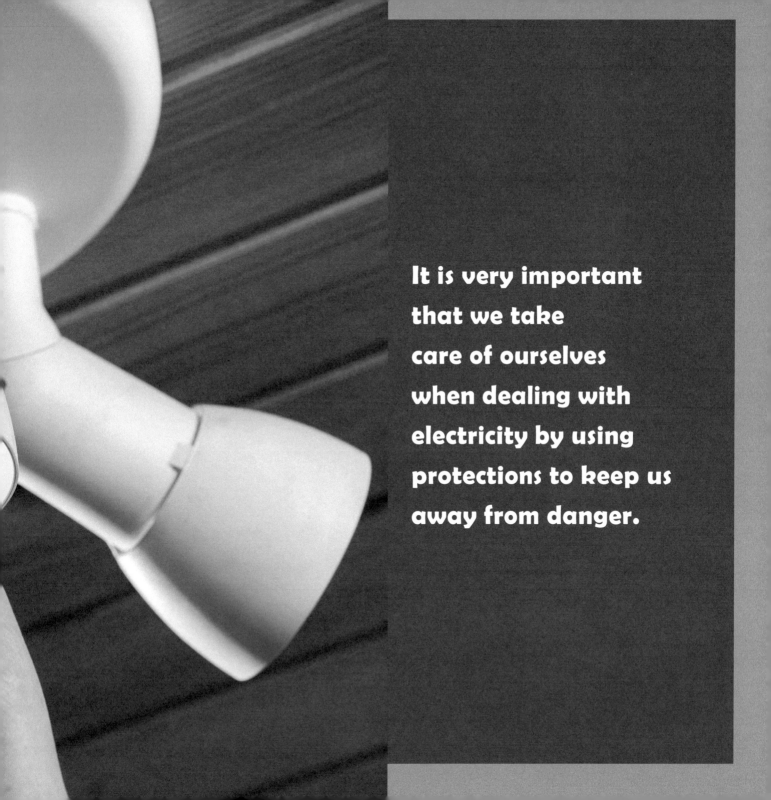

It is very important
that we take
care of ourselves
when dealing with
electricity by using
protections to keep us
away from danger.

Visit

BABY PROFESSOR
EDUCATION KIDS

www.BabyProfessorBooks.com

to download Free Baby Professor eBooks
and view our catalog of new and exciting
Children's Books

Made in the USA
Thornton, CO
05/14/24 13:03:40

1760deba-87a9-4024-8e0f-bc5420f9c2f5R01